GW00319377

It's Just Not Father's Day!

Published in 2012 by Prion
an imprint of the Carlton Publishing Group
20 Mortimer Street
London W1T 3JW

10 9 8 7 6 5 4 3 2 1

ISBN 978-1-85375-840-9

A CIP catalogue record of this book can be obtained from the British Library.

Printed in Dubai

The publishers would like to thank the following sources for their kind permission to reproduce the pictures in this book:

Getty Images: /H Armstrong Roberts/Retrofile: 9, 16, 70, 102; /Constance Bannister Corp: 77; /George Douglas/Picture Post: 6; /Fox Photos: 13, 22; /Bert Hardy/Picture Post: 42; /Hulton Archive: 49; /Mark Kauffman/Time & Life Pictures: 94; /Keystone View/FPG: 33; /Keystone-France/Gamma-Keystone: 122; /Harold M Lambert/Lambert: 30, 39; /George Marks/Retrofile: 25, 58, 61, 66, 101, 105, 109, 126; /Picture Post/Hulton Archive: 82; /Popperfoto: 14; /Joseph Scherschel/Time & Life Pictures: 93; /SuperStock: 74, 86, 89, 110, 114, 118, 125; /Three Lions: 45; /George S Zimbel: 54
iStockphoto.com: 21, 34, 41, 46, 78

Thinkstock: /Comstock: 62, 85, 97; /Creatas: 98; /Fuse: 65; /Goodshoot: 73; /Hemera: 10, 113, 117; / Image Source Pink: 18; /Ingram Publishing: 50; /iStockphoto: 53, 106, 128; /Lifesize: 29, 90; /Monkey Business Images Ltd: 121; /Pixland: 69, 81; /Stockbyte: 26, 57

It's Just Not Father's Day!

The challenges of being a dad

Peter Stake

PRION

Fatherhood

One day you're out every night with the lads, not a care in the world. Then suddenly you've got a ring on your finger, a shopping trolley full of disposable nappies and no money in your wallet. Say goodbye to those boozy late nights – you'll be lucky if you can tell the *difference* between day and night once you've experienced the joys of sleep deprivation – courtesy of a pair of tiny but unbelievably powerful lungs.

But don't worry about that, because it only gets worse. Before you know it, your little bundles of poop have learned to walk and talk, and are growing out of every item of clothing you buy them. Then you can look forward to the joys of school (and you thought you'd seen the back of grumpy teachers!), teenage tantrums, driving lessons and university! And all the time you'll be thinking, "surely I never gave *my* parents this much grief!"

Just remember that you're still a bloke and no one's going to listen to you whine, least of all your fellow dads. Your only chance of staying sane is to see the funny side, which is why I made this book. Basically it's a collection of dad-related pictures with some stupid captions. But, hopefully, it will give you a chuckle in one of those rare moments when you can actually hear yourself think.

Peter Stake, father of two and still (mostly) sane

Dad wondered if the kids would notice the subtle aftertaste of bathroom grouter in the spaghetti.

**Mother saw the kids
as a sort of science experiment.
Father refused to partake
in such bat-shittery.**

'Paternity leave' is for wimps.

The girls had been pampering Dad for days. Soon he would crack and the pony would be theirs.

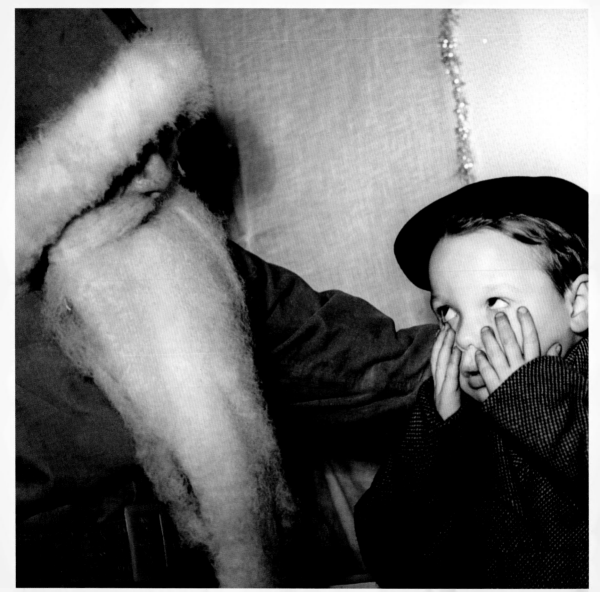

"Dad, you are seriously creeping me out – give me my bloody present or I'm calling Child Line."

**Fatherhood is an education.
Dad held a marriage certificate,
three birth certificates
and a Master's Degree
in going round the bend.**

"Honour thy father."
Exodus 20:12

"Whatever."
Luke, 8 and a half

"It's a picture of you getting angry and demonstrating your characteristic lack of art appreciation, Daddy."

Emily wanted to be a hair stylist
when she grew up and
greatly appreciated Dad's
participation in her training.

"Oh that's charming – you've given my dinner to the dog? Have you any idea how much a new dog costs?"

"Dad, your stocks have just dropped ten points and you've got milk on your tie."

**Remember the days when
you could enjoy an agonizing
Sunday morning hangover
in peace?**

**Having twins is indescribable...
a bit like being kicked between
the legs and losing *both* balls.**

"Dad, it's okay.
If you don't know where
Europe is, just say so."

"For goodness sake James,
if you're going to let Claire
practice jujitsu on you, can you
please do it outside!"

The man-eating pine tree would make this an unforgettable Christmas.

**Dad's attempts to feed
little Russell were pathetic,
so Russell felt a bit of remedial
training was in order.**

**Mum felt slightly bad
that Dad would blame the kids
for her response to his 'night out
with the lads'.**

"Jennifer, I think Daddy's had enough waterboarding for one day."

Dad didn't see the point
of wandering around the park
if Tom was going to sleep
through the whole excursion.
Actually maybe that wasn't
such a bad idea....

Girls often develop an aesthetic appreciation early in life. Gemma had no doubt that Daddy's face could benefit from some surgical enhancement.

"Daddy, are you staying in our room because Mummy's aunty is coming to visit?"

In the event of domestic apocalypse, assume the position shown and wait for things to calm down.

**"Dad, I hate beards.
Can't you take a bloody hint?"**

Dad still couldn't figure out why Mum was immune to the nerve-gas stench of freshly-filled nappy.

Selina was not happy
with her birthday present.
She'd asked for an AK-47 and a
box of fragmentation grenades.

When your paternal authority is questioned, assume the position shown and wait for things to calm down.

Dad's idea of issuing junk bonds (instead of pocket money) was inspired, if unpopular.

Extortion (n).
A rare instance of communication
from one's teenage offspring.

"Damn, I'm so tanked.
Cheers, Dad –
you're my besht mate."

If your prolonged contemplation of another female's anatomy is remarked upon, assume the position shown and wait for things to calm down.

"How many times do I have to say I'm sorry I said your boyfriend looked like Lady Gaga?"

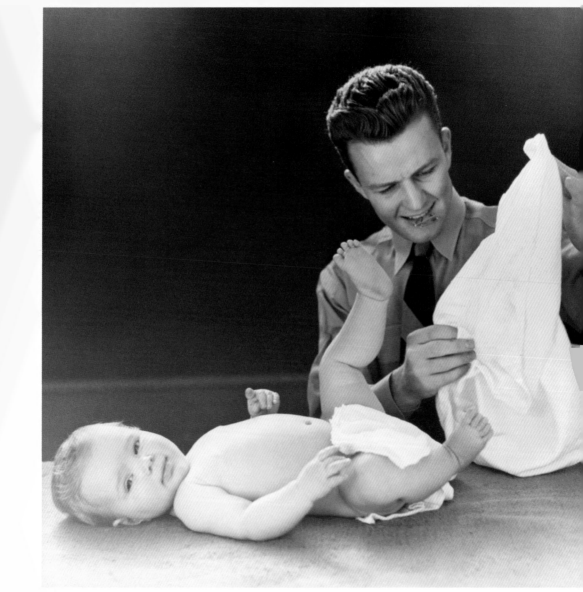

Another day, another opportunity
to ponder "wtf?"

"Yeah, I'm sorry, I wouldn't normally call you but my wife knows bugger-all about car maintenance."

"It says that you work very hard at being an underachiever."

**"Woah, Dad!
That looks suspiciously
like the stuff I left in my potty
five minutes ago."**

The French philosopher
Pierre-Joseph Proudhon said:
"property is theft."

**Please note that fully
comprehensive car insurance
does not cover counselling for
posttraumatic stress disorder.**

The family had always
prided itself in a high level
of literacy. But sometimes Dad
wished the kids would just sod off
and vandalize the garden.

You split an atom and can annihilate an entire city.

Funny how tiny things sometimes have such a devastating effect on life.

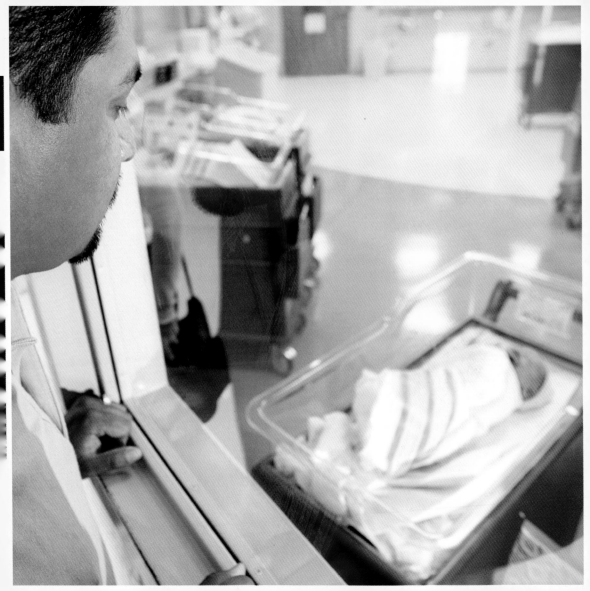

Mum insisted that her weekly consumption of ten bottles of Chardonnay was purely medicinal.

"I don't care if I *do* call your mother that from time to time, you'll treat the dog with more respect!"

**Remember when your mates
used to do this after
one Sambuca too many?**

It seemed funnier back then.

**Some days all you want is a
time machine and a
home vasectomy kit.**

Dad's rodeo game was excellent because it broke at least 17 Health and Safety laws.

**Ah, the good old days...
when corporal punishment was
known as 'practical parenting'.**

"Dad, if you keep making me laugh I'm going to poop myself again."

"Daddy, please. My stupid brother might have bought into your non-existent securities market – but I'd prefer cash."

"Daddy, you can do better than that. How would someone motivate *you* to eat a spoonful of cold snot?"

It was one of those
life-changing moments.
Dad saw his entire bank balance
flash before his eyes.

Hello fatherhood.
Goodbye promotion.

When informed that your punctuality at mealtimes is less than satisfactory, assume the position shown and wait for things to calm down.

The stylish new suite that
Mum had chosen would have
made any family of hobbits proud.

**"Holy shit, Dad!
How many times do I have to tell
you to activate the parent lock?"**

At just six years of age Pamela was ready to take over her father's role – as chief enforcer for the Sicilian Mafia.

**"I'll tell you later.
I'm still being stalked by the
Boyfriend Police."**

**Dad loved the office,
it was the only place he could
actually get some peace.**

**Nothing says 'trust'
like a Facebook chaperone.**

"Isn't it funny how your mother always has one of her bad heads after it's been raining?"

"Miss said you got all my last homework wrong!"

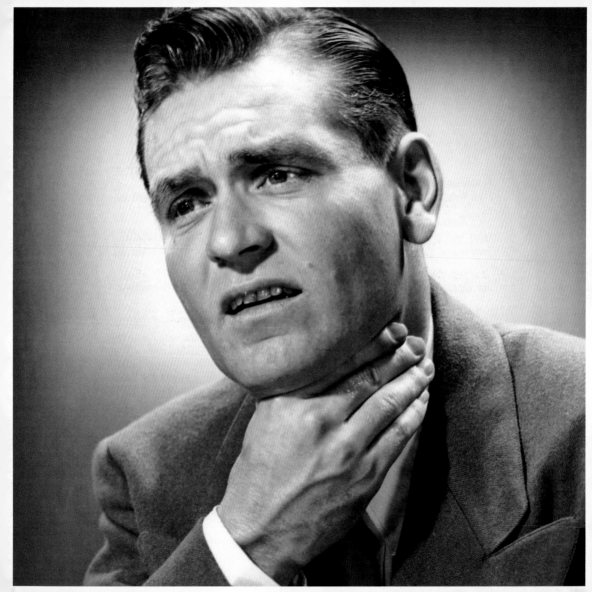

Never lie to your spouse. When asked whether an item of apparel causes her posterior to appear out of proportion, it is perfectly acceptable to develop acute laryngitis.